The Open Gate to Paradise: A Lifeline for the Wrongfully Convicted and Their Families

Dedicated to Archie Williams, an Exoneree

By Lindy Morelli RMCH

Lighthouse of Scranton
P.O. 199 Scranton, PA 18504
www.sacredlighthouse.org

I0143181

Preface:

The purpose of this book is to give hope, guidance, and comfort to the wrongly convicted and their families. If you or your loved one find yourself in this situation, if you feel despair, trapped,and overwhelmed with insurmountable burdens, this book is for you. In it, you will find answers and strategies for thriving. If you have an open heart, you will also find a way to be truly happy.

May God bless you, as you read, with grace and peace.

Sincerely,
From my heart to yours,
Lindy Morelli RMCH
Friend of a wrongly convicted person.

Prologue
"Lazarus Come Forth"

Note: I have used the Biblical story of Lazarus, from the Gospel of John chapter 11 as a backdrop, and as a theme of what this story is all about. Lazarus was dead, but he was brought back to life. In my heart and mind, that is what has happened to me in my personal journey of loving and fighting for someone, who is wrongly convicted. Maybe if you take some time to meditate on this Gospel story, you will understand my story of transformation more clearly, and the same thing may surely happen for you.

Table of Contents

Chapter One
When Your World is Turned Upside down

(Summary of my Personal Story)

Note: Names and places have been omitted or changed to protect the identity of individuals.

How do I begin to tell this story? I feel I need to tell you something about myself and myexperience of dealing with a wrongful conviction on a day-to-day basis, and about how it is for me, standing by someone who is suffering this firsthand. But, how on earth do I begin to tell it, since I could write volumes about the circumstances, my feelings, the struggles, etc.?

I don't think you need volumes, since you surely have volumes of your own, which are similar to mine, but I will at least tell you the basics so you can have confidence in what you are going to read in these pages, and so that you are completely assured that I truly understand.

I met Damien eight years ago through a prayer community called the Carmelites. The Carmelites are a worldwide Catholic prayer community of people who are dedicated to anintense inner life of love and prayer in allegiance to Jesus Christ as Lord and God. (Well, anyway, I thought you might want to know who and what we are all about.) But back to our story: Damien wanted to find someone with whom to have spiritual fellowship, and he wrote to the national office of the Carmelite Study Institute in Washington DC to see if they could find him a spiritual companion who would be able to offer spiritual support according to the Carmelite tradition.

So he wrote to me in March of 2014. At the time, I had been working in prison ministry for over 30 years and had founded Lighthouse in Scranton, which is a ministry organization whose main purpose is to help people who are "falling through the cracks"; to provide comfort, hope, and guidance to persons in need.

For many years prior to meeting Damien, I had worked with the poor and with people from all walks of life. Also I had been deeply immersed in the lives and pains of incarcerated people. Many people had come to Lighthouse to live upon being released, and I empathized and supported them through their struggles. However, I had never known or loved a wrongly convicted person until I met someone from up here in my hometown of Scranton, Pennsylvania, whose name was Cory.

Cory had been in on a false conviction of murder due to a forced false confession.

When he got out, he wrote a book about his harrowing, disgraceful experience with the justice system. Needless to say, I have great respect for the many good, honest people who work in the justice system. But it need not be pointed out that surely, for the many grave, unconscionable errors, and wrongs that occur, something needs to be done and to be written about.

5

Never, in all my years of working in prison ministry, had I heard about a wrongful conviction. I know that is hard to believe, but I certainly didn't make a habit of asking folks about their cases. I knew it must have occurred, and it saddens me now to think that someone, orseveral persons, might have been in that situation and I didn't help them. But, for whatever reason, in any case, I never met anyone in that situation that I knew of. So, when I read Cory's book it turned my life upside down.

I became physically sick from reading it, but still, even this did not prepare me, when I got to know Damien, for what we would be up against. In the midst of our writing letters, we discovered that God had a plan. We became spiritual friends and began working together on ministry projects. In getting to know Damien, I could see the purity of his heart and his Christ- like qualities. I knew he was completely honest and real. That is why we became friends. That iswhy I said yes to the call of becoming Damien's advocate.

It is impossible to express the gratitude and passion I feel in having received this calling, both to fight for the wrongly convicted and to write this book. This is all God's work, and my life is all God's. I have no regrets for the suffering this fight, thus far, has caused me. On the contrary, I have only joy and thankfulness, but more about that later. (No, I'm not crazy.) But anyway, back to the point, let me just tell you; it has cost me my life in pursuing this fight for Damien.

Within a year of starting to work on the case, which included interviewing witnessesfrom twenty years ago (it was twenty years ago at the time; it is now twenty-eight years), diggingup evidence, raising money for investigators, finding forensic experts, and getting way in overmy head-- into something I had no prior knowledge of-- well, let's just say I became very sick, and the illness from stress, which grew worse as the years went by, grew so severe that I couldn'tfunction at all. But I'll get back to that.

I remember the first time I called an investigator. When he told me it would cost ten thousand dollars just to look at all the case materials, I almost collapsed right on the spot. By thistime, I had been advocating for Damien for about a year. I had been flying back and forth to another state from Pennsylvania, nearly monthly, to see Damien and to give support to his mother.

My nervous system couldn't handle the pain and grief, and I began waking up in a cold sweat nightly, remaining in a perpetual state of extreme terror from that point on. Every time Damien would call, I would go into a panic. Every little thing about his being in prison shattered me. It crushed me. If I were eating a nice salad with fresh vegetables, or if I were outside on a nice sunny day among the beautiful trees and flowers, my heart would break with grief because I simply couldn't believe or fathom that Damien wasn't here. Why had he lost so much, when Ihad been given so much? I felt such guilt and grief. There was no end in sight.

I couldn't believe that he hadn't had a cucumber in twenty years, or strawberries, or that all the little things in life that were so easy for me on the outside he had been deprived of for decades. Everything he couldn't have made my life bitter and empty. It was as if I could feel the cruelty of prison in my bones. I had terrible dreams about it at night, and would wake up shaking, feeling as if, I myself had been dragged through the streets, beaten, shackled, and brought to nothing. Rage. Anguish, stultifying sorrow. I felt like I was suffocating to death.

Even more, pain upon pain, ravaging my soul, knowing that this scenario was being repeated in thousands, maybe millions of families, throughout the world, and that this travesty was happening countless numbers of times, for innocent people who had been tortured and hauled offto prison, even though in actual fact they were not guilty of the crimes for which they had been convicted.

Well, there are no words for the agony I felt, as if it were happening to me! What could I do? How would Damien ever get out? How would anyone get out? How could such colossal evil go unchecked! I didn't know the answer, but I was going to fight. For starters, I was determined to help, in whatever ways I could, one person at a time: I wasn't going to quit, till Damien was free.

I really believed that we would get things resolved quickly. I just hung on by my fingernails, thinking that it would be done in a few months. But oh! The shock and sadness, a train wreck in my soul, never could I have known, how wrong I was!

The first year, I baked bread. I'd carefully pack some away in the freezer. How excited I was, bolstering up my hopes. I called it Good Faith Bread, thinking that in a few months Damien would be out, finally free.

I got a little silver box and put all my extra change in the box, sure that he would be homelater that year, and everything would work out fine, but as I said, I was naïve. My heart was simple, and pure. My hopes were destroyed.

We looked online for a lawyer. He had good ratings, so I trusted him. Believe me, that was a very bad idea. For four years we went through tortuous hell, because he absolutelywouldn't communicate with me. He ignored texts, certified letters, phone calls, and everything.

He simply let the case sit on his desk for nine months at a time without us hearing anything from him. Of course, this made things much worse, until, one day, finally, I told Damien that after four years of this torture we had to get another lawyer or I was quitting everything. I would not have done that, but I was desperate enough to say it.

Since this all began, eight years ago, I was diagnosed with adrenal insufficiency. My body just couldn't keep up with the amount of stress put on it. The weakness, utter exhaustion, and sickness is impossible to describe. Severe trauma had depleted all my reserves.

Two years ago, when I made my last trip to see him, before the Coronavirus started, I couldn't walk through the airport due to weakness, and I had to be wheeled to the gate in a wheelchair. I couldn't eat for almost two years, and lived on protein shakes, chicken broth and apple juice. My nervous system was shot. I couldn't talk, go out, listen to music, read a book, or be around people. I couldn't even have conversations about everyday things, because the exertion and stress just to interact about anything, or put effort into anything, was too much stress on my body. Too much noise, stimulation, and pain, trauma or stress would push my bloodpressure down to a dangerously low number, or make my pulse go up too high. I couldn't concentrate on anything.

I had to lie in bed most of the day. I went to two special medical doctors. They are integrative and holistic doctors. They prescribed several different kinds of vitamins and herbs, because I didn't want to get on regular medication for stress, such as anti-anxiety drugs, or anything like steroids for the adrenal insufficiency. I simply didn't have the physical and emotional resources to go on coping with this ongoing stress. The doctors told me I needed complete rest, quiet, and no stress. I couldn't engage in regular conversations with anyone, and everything was too much for me, even making a salad, doing one load of laundry or anything. Even walking around the block, going to a store, or walking up a flight of steps was extremely difficult for me.

Everything hurt in my body and soul. My muscles ached. I had to go to the chiropractor for my neck and back twice a week, and to physical therapy for my feet, because I couldn't standor walk for more than fifteen minutes. I would get three or four migraine headaches a week, depending on how stressful things were that week. I was nauseous most of the time, and food is still sometimes repulsive. My body and mind became so depleted that the doctors told me that if there was a place I could go to in the country, with good food, fresh air, quiet and peaceful surroundings, like the old-fashioned sanitoriums that tuberculosis patients went to in the past, they would have sent me there.

But, since such places don't exist in our day, I had to make my home and my surroundings into a place of complete rest and solitude. I had to go through a whole revamping of my way of life, of the way I thought, and the way I lived my life. It has been like building myself up from the ground up, or coming back from the dead, since I didn't have the inner amounts of physical stamina to walk, or think, or move or anything.

My nervous system felt like someone had hit me with a Mack truck, or like I was being dragged around and mutilated by a high-speed train. Day by day, I was disintegrating physically. "Are you going to die, Lin?" my sister Liv asked one day. I could hear the grief and terror in her voice. Helpless, she was beside herself. Just imagine her anguish, since we are twins.

At the time of this writing, I am still in the healing process. Recently, I got Covid, and was diagnosed with chronic Lyme's disease. Day to day, my health is a balancing act, since depending on how much sleep I can get, and on many other factors, I feel quite sick off and on, through the day, and have more or less energy. Even a pleasant thing can be too stressful, since I am in a weakened state, so I must be careful, pace myself and go slow. Emotionally, when this all started, I didn't have the ability to cope. Believe me, talking to people didn't help. In fact, it only made things worse, and my world got smaller and smaller. I just felt isolated and alone.

Once, I called someone whose husband had been in for 30 some years. He had been released, and his name had been cleared. "Your friend might never get out. He might die there, said. "So, you better chill out. Calm down." "I accept that," I said without missing a beat. Yet, a bomb had blown up in my soul.

11

Talking to therapists didn't help after a while either. There were no magic words to make the pain go away. Besides, it wasn't just the pain of the case. It was the pain of my whole life, which had been quite difficult. I simply couldn't get relief, that is, until I went to some doctors and therapists who truly understand trauma, which can only be healed through the grace of God. Therapies such as biofeedback and somatic therapy, are the only things that truly helped me heal,since those types of therapies can help a person release the trauma that gets stored in a person's body. The therapists told me that I was like a shell-shocked person who had been to war. I was still in a war. They said that I wasn't just burned-out. I was "burned through."

Through the years, I had to learn to think all over again. I had to learn to think the right thoughts; to retrain my mind; to think differently with true faith and hope. I had to learn to put complete faith in God alone. That is the only thing that has given me peace.

One day, after six years of severe struggle, waking up daily in a frantic state, and workingnonstop at breakneck speed, it dawned on me that maybe, just maybe, I could try to go on with my life and not focus so much on the case, since I had done all I could, but it was still hard.
I remember the day I went out to play in a handbell choir one Sunday. Another day I went out toa quilting group, just to try to get my mind on something else. I felt shaky and sick. My heart wasn't in it. But I couldn't stay immobilized any longer. I had no control over what was going to happen. I didn't want to continue to die emotionally.

Panic. Bitterness. Crushing work. I was close to death. Then, slowly, I came to realize that I had done all I could. So, no matter how shattered and terrified I was, I was going to try to let go and trust God. I was going to try to go on with my life here at home, six hundred miles away from Damien.

Yet even though I had reached this conclusion, for several years my life was nothing but going to doctors and trying all kinds of healing therapies. Terror-stricken about money, I had no idea how I was going to pay for all the lawyers, investigators, Damien's expenses, traveling back and forth, my deteriorating health, all the bills of keeping Lighthouse going, etc.

My hair even fell out completely, through all of this, even though I tried all the goofy things they say to do online so it wouldn't. I was scrubbing my head with coconut oil, egg yolk, lemon juice, green tea, etc., but nothing worked. Lo and behold, there I was, bald as can be. Ugh! Oh, well. You might as well laugh. It is better than being too sad.

Actually, that is one thing Damien taught me. You might as well joke and find the bright side of things, or you will die in this process. Indeed, there is still hope, and in these pages I will tell you how that can still be, and where to find it. As I write this, I am progressing on this journey, and these pages are about what I have, and am learning, as I move forward toward a bright future. "A bright future?", you might say. "How can you say that, if you practically died, and there is no end in sight for Damien's release!"

Well, if you read on, you will see what has happened to me, and what is happening to me now, so that I have gone from nearly dying through all of this to a person who is truly thriving and happy. God bless you as you read these pages. May you persevere in getting to the other sideof whatever prison walls you are facing, be they actual prison walls or symbolic. May you grow stronger day by day, and may God hold your hand and help you to thrive.

By the way, just as a little postscript, so that you will really know you are reading the thoughts of a true friend and ally. Here is a poem I wrote soon after I realized that I was called to stand by Damien, and others, come what may.

This is my rejoicing song.

From my heart to yours:
God is our hope and life.
God is our solution.
God is our beginning and our end.
Hallelujah!

For the Sake of Love
By Lindy Morelli RMCH
Written August 2014

When cold grief comes,
She sits right down.
She makes her home

Inside your soul—

She settles in—

There, spreading out her massive skirts,

Which smother you, like a thick, heavy blanket,

Pushing down; down; down.

Her boney fingers, digging in—

Her icy hands go 'round your neck—

She cuts off breath,

And every hope of life.

Oh, just be still, my pounding heart;

Don't question why it has to be;

Just let the waves of sorrow roll

Over your throbbing soul.

Breathe in;

Breathe out.

Breathe in;

Breathe out,

Lest you begin to drown,

Beneath the water's cruel, relentless force.

Just cling;

Just cling;

Just cling to hope,

Though you are sick and weak,
That someday, soon your soul will be set free.

Then rescued from all pain and loss,
From suffocating grief,
May Christ, his clear,
And suffering eyes, see,
His arms, alone,
Your solace, refuge be.

In Jesus, may you daily walk
In burning love and bliss,
And in His presence of delight,
On His vast love, subsist.

Mary, my mother,
Comfort, rest
Your tenderness, secure
Accompany us, in all duress,
Be our foundation, sure.

Have trust my heart,
Have trust my heart,
Though strangled by life's grief;
Your faith in God will carry you

And bring your soul's release.

Be still, my heart.
Don't try to find
The why of this or that,
For God, alone,
Can still the killing
Storm.

Just a little note, so we can move forward into the rest of this book:

So, where do you find yourself, dear friend and reader, after digesting all of that? You are digging down deep. That's where you find yourself, when your life has no evident purpose. Pray for grace and strength, if you are at the end of your rope. Pray with sincerity, and truly believe, even if you can muster only the tiniest bit of faith. And for family members, just for a little distraction, if you feel up to it, look online for mustard seeds. Why not order yourself a packet? You can use them to flavor chicken and simple salads. See how little they are? And you can even use them for something nice, even though they are so little. Are you surprised? A mustard seed isn't that big. Isn't it neat how something so little can be used for something so good?

And for you guys and girls in prison, use your imagination; write a poem about making something out of nothing. Start with a bunch of words about little things and nothing and see where the word picture goes. You will also be surprised about how little things can grow. Try it. You

17

might like it. You might even have fun.

Chapter Two
So Now What?

What do you do now? You find yourself in hell. Everything is swirling, like a typhoon. No one is with you. You are numb, in shock. Where do you turn? How will you ever get out? You can't. You just can't. You can't make it all go away. You have no purpose, no hope. You think you'd be better off dead. But, if you let yourself go down the tubes, the system will have won. So, just on the basis of pure logic, you've got to convince yourself that you have to get up and keep on going.

"But how? Where?", you ask, as you thrash around your cell. Well, maybe not literally, but still... Suddenly your life, as you knew it, is gone. Sinking, gasping for breath, you are goingto drown. Oh! How I wish I could alleviate this pain, like a bridge over troubled water, if I could.

Breathe. Just breathe. Breathe in. Breathe out. You breathe. Just breathe. Say to yourself: "Now I'm breathing in. I'm breathing out." Put all your concentration into it now, so you don't go crazy or kill yourself. Breathing is hard, though. Everything is hard. But, right now, breathing is all you have.

Just keep on breathing in. Breathe out. Breathe in. Breathe out. Breathe in. Breathe out. Put all your effort into it. Shut everything else out. Feel the breath going into your body. Then feel all the stress going out, as you exhale. Make your out-breaths longer than your in- breaths, so you don't hyperventilate. Then, push your feet into the floor. Feel your feet. They are being held up. The ground underneath you isn't falling apart, or shaking, like everything else. The amazing thing about this is that the prison floor, made of concrete, under your feet is firm. It's steady, secure. It's a blessing. How ironic, but true.

You might be wondering why I am writing about breathing, and why I am writing about the prison floor under your feet. This chapter is supposed to be about coping with this mess, isn'tit? So, it might seem irrelevant or stupid. But to start by simply breathing, and in really grounding yourself by using the solid concrete under your feet, by consistently focusing on these two things, that is how you are going to make it through this. I know it feels hopeless though. You are trapped. What can you do? How can you even begin to find your way out.

Tmore you think about it, the sicker you feel. You can't sleep. You can't eat. It's as if you've been shot through with poison. You can't get relief, no matter what you do. The systemis out to kill you in one fell swoop. Believe me, for us who are on the outside it is a type of hell also.

All I thought about for years was Damien, on the other side of those hideous walls, surrounded by stench and violence. I felt as if I were in prison too, and probably so do any of your family members or loved ones who are supporting you, who are not running away, and whohave the courage to stick it out. For us, the added bitter complication is that we can't do anythingimmediately to get you out. So, not only do we feel, taste, see, and hear the anguish that is all around you, but we feel helpless!

We absolutely MUST find a way to get you out! So, for now, you and me, so we don't go crazy, or quit altogether, let's just breathe. In and out. In and out.

Yes, go back to that concrete under your feet, and feel how good it is that you are not sinking, or disintegrating, even if you think you are. All that is here now, is your breath, and this concrete, and this book which you are holding in your hands.

Chapter Three
Why Should I Care?
(Self-Care)

Self-care: "What on earth does that mean?" "Self-care...what's that? Who cares abouttaking care of myself anyway?" "I am dying, drowning," you may say. "Why even bother!
There is no hope as long as I am here, and there is no hope as long as my loved one is inside." But the fact of the matter is, first of all, dear family member, if you don't take care of yourself,your loved one inside will have no one to rely on, no connection with the outside world, and noresources from which to draw to get out of this hell, so you absolutely have to start taking care ofyourself, whether you want to or not, and you must start doing it now.

Also, my dear friend, for you who are on the inside, remember to breathe, and realize thatyou have got to take care of yourself too, because if you give up now, and let yourself just die and go to pot, you will die losing, and no one will ever know the truth, that you are innocent of this crime and you do not deserve to be there.

No, you don't!! Go ahead, get angry!! Think about what you are doing if you just let yourself die and drown and sink. You are giving in. You must not, under any circumstances, do that! You have to decide here and now, that you are not going to let this suffocating mess, this hell, this anger, this sense of drowning kill you. You are going to catch the lifeline which I am throwing you, you're going to fight, you are going to survive, and you are going to make it.

You don't know how, right now, but you are going to.

Here's what you've got to do. Now come on! Commit yourself! Make a choice and do it. I am doing it on the outside for my friend Damien, for all of you, and for God. Now you have gotto do it for yourself and for your divine purpose.

Here is what you must do every day. Make a choice to live. Yes, choose to live! You maysay to yourself, "How the hell am I going to do that, while in here? This is a death trap." Yes, butyou have to decide to live. If you don't decide it, no one can decide it for you. You have to getup every day and decide to live. You have to breathe in and breathe out. You have to realize and take this to heart: All you have to cope with is this moment. Not tomorrow, not yesterday, when this terrible thing fell upon you. You have to live through this moment. You might as well make it as good as it can be, as long as you are here now in this moment, and where you are, because otherwise, you are making the hell for yourself worse. When you don't accept the reality of your situation, and the moment as it is, you become overwhelmed and you start sinking, so just breathe, and accept this moment as it is.

Just practice this and practice it through every moment. Yes, this practicing to live in the moment also applies to you, dear beloved friends and family of the wrongly convicted, becauseif you don't accept reality as it is, you will check out, abandon your loved one, run away, or distract

23

yourself so much that you end up hurting your loved one more than they are alreadyhurt. No, you don't have to like it. You also have to get angry at injustice, and do something to mobilize your anger enough to be a resource for your loved one.

So, here's what you do. Wrongly convicted individuals that are on the way to justice, andbeloved family and friends: Get angry and start finding healthy ways to deal with it. Write it all down. Start writing in a journal every day. You have plenty of time if you are inside, and this will help you clear your head. If you can, do some vigorous exercise. That will help you deal with anger and the strong emotions.

If you are on the outside, you may feel too sick and overwhelmed to do it, but no matter how either of you feel, you still have to eventually get out of bed, because you will starve lying there, and you will have to eventually get up and go to the bathroom, or drink some water or something, so just get up and start moving your body. Start walking around your cell, or your house. Go out for a walk and breathe. Write your feelings down. Yes, I know, it is hard when you are in prison, because no one can see your anger, or grief, and you can't confide in anyone, but you can confide in me, and you can confide in God. So, do these three things every single day. Get up. Eat. Drink, walk, move your body, and write your feelings down. Develop a routine that includes the following things.

Physical self-care: eating as many vegetables as you can find. Yeah, I know, you might not like them. They might be watery or unappealing, but eat them anyway, because some day you are getting out, and you have to keep your organs and muscles strong. Yeah, yeah, yeah, youmay say. How do you know I am getting out? They have double murder on my head, so what areyou talking about. Well, just do it, and keep a bright hope alive for the future. Fight and fight for justice and peace and eat your veggies while you are at it! Besides eating, just move your body.

Exercise every day, even if you are stuck in your cell.

Also, don't forget that goofy breathing technique I told you about and pushing your feet into the concrete floor, so your body gets the message you are not drowning or dead yet. You might wish you were, but there you go again. You have the power to choose, so choose life, so the devil and the corrupt justice system you got messed over with, doesn't win.

Now, besides taking care of yourself physically, for the people on the inside, and familiesand friends, you have to take care of yourself emotionally. Since you are in prison, you can't trust anyone, but you can trust me, so write me a letter and I will help you. You will find my address in the front of this book. Write in a journal and then rip it up or send it out. Write poetry, draw a picture, write a story, or do something to express yourself in whatever ways you can. Same for you family members. If you are freaking out like I was for the past several years, find a counselor, or someone to talk to, or call me. You will find my number in the front of this book.

So, besides taking care of yourselves physically and emotionally, you have to find some spirituality. Yes, something to believe in. You might be religious. You might not. Either way, that doesn't matter. The research shows that anyone who makes it through any tragedy or overwhelming trauma (which this definitely is, wouldn't you say?), they have something to believe in. They find some meaning.

Look in the prison library for the book *Man's Search for Meaning*, and you will see what I mean. If you can't get it, write me and I will get it for you. You have got to find something to believe in, and something to hang on to. It could just be the hope of getting out. That is okay to start with, if you can't start anywhere else. You family members have to do the same thing.

Now listen, part of self-care is doing what you can to change your situation. So, get the book *Company of Giants* by Rama Dev Jager or *Win Your Case* by Gerry Spence, and have it sent to you. You can also get the book on how to make successful negotiations. It is called *Getting Past No* by William Ury. If you can't get it, let me know and I will get it for you. But first try to get it yourself though, because money doesn't grow on trees. (Smile.)

Anyway, start studying your case and learning the law. You have to be an expert in your own case and in your own freedom. Learn the law. Don't depend on your lawyers to get youout. Do it yourself.

Now besides taking care of yourself, physically, emotionally, and spiritually, and legally, you have to find a way to live a meaningful life in prison. Yeah, I know. That sounds crazy but look around. People are doing it just to survive. And please don't say that they can doit because

26

they are not wrongly convicted. I know that is surely a tempting way to think, and it is true, that they don't have the same horrible unjust evil situation you do, but you still have to do itfor yourself! Please do it! Get involved in whatever you can. Just do it, because it will make yourdays better and more tolerable. Do it and let me know how it goes.

Special note to friends and family; mobilize yourself, think of what you need. You can't save your loved one if you are drowning. Do what I am saying. If you have some money, yeah, I know, you probably already emptied out all your bank accounts if you had them…obviously, youare going to spend all your money to get a lawyer, but if you don't have money, check out the Innocence Project online, and send your loved one their address.

Remember, you have to do the things to take care of yourself too, so if you weren't in thehabit of it like me before this all started, you have to start developing a game plan to keep yourself healthy, physically, emotionally, and spiritually, so you can be there for your loved one, and stay alive for the rest of your life. Life; you must want it, and true life you must have in the best and fullest way possible!

You have two choices: either you stand by your loved one or you don't. Unfortunately, most people check out of the situation, because they can't stand the helplessness and pain.

Because, believe it or not, for family and friends of the wrongly convicted it might be even compounded with pain, because not only do you have the fact that you loved one is there and all that entails, physically, emotionally and spiritually, which I don't have to tell you about since you are in it now, like me, but you have to carry the responsibilities and burdens of your life out there; like if you have other children to care for, or a sick relative, or a job, or whatever.

You have to support your loved one inside and do all the stuff outside, while carrying the burden of this injustice on your shoulders and the sense of great helplessness you may feel. That is why, family and friends, you have to have faith. You have to also have something or someone to believe in.

I am a Catholic, Christian and I believe in Jesus as Lord and God. I believe in the Holy Trinity and in the love and goodness and mercy of God! Get strong mentally, spiritually and emotionally. If you need help, get it. You are dealing with a very serious thing, that unless someone has lived through, they won't understand. Most people, when you tell them about it, will probably turn away, scoff or say something discouraging like, "Well, if he or she isinnocent, why is he or she still there?" Don't listen to anyone. Don't talk to anyone except someone who really is supportive. Stay away from negativity. This is good advice for whether you are inside or outside. Pump yourself up with good positive things. Negativity will killyou. Get rid of it. Put positive things in your mind. Negativity is poison. Do things to nourish yourself. Go out in nature. Do something to comfort yourself. Here are some ideas that may help:Hold a warm drink in your hand, even if it is just hot water from the sink. Hold the cup and feel its warmth. Let it comfort you. Find a nature program on television. Enjoy the scenery. Picture yourself outside in nature, even if you can't go there now. You need to use your imagination

28

to lift yourself up. Go outside whenever you can and breathe in the fresh air. Let it revive you.

I hope the suggestions in these chapter help. If you have any more why not send me a

letter.

Chapter Four
Build Something Beautiful

(Creativity)

Creativity? What is that! You may be asking that in amazement. Now I know you feel like you have nothing inside, nothing left to give, but eventually, you must get up, even if it is just to eat, or drink, or for roll call, so since you have to get up for that, you may as well find out how-to live in prison. Yeah, I said "live," not just survive, or curse every moment of everyday. Live? You may ask, how can I do that?

Well, one key thing that will help you for sure is for you to realize that you have gifts inside of you. You still have something to give, and even though this all is happening to you, youdidn't lose all of that. You were put here on this planet for a reason. You don't see it now, but you were. You may be saying: "What do you mean? I can't see any reason for this mess, and I don't see any purpose," but believe me, you were put on this planet for a reason, and you know better than anyone that evil exists in the world. Sin exists, and darkness exists, but the best wayto curse the darkness is not to join it by sinking down in despair and negativity, but to bring light into it.

A famous person once said that the best way to curse the darkness is to light one single candle. So, what you have to do is figure out how you can do that in your daily life, right where you are now. You have something to give, like no one else. You are in a prime place where you are surrounded by fellow sufferers, and you can do something good. You can help yourself by using your gifts. If you like to sing, sing. If you like to draw, draw. If you like to write, write.

If you like to tell jokes, tell jokes. Well, you get the picture. Find a creative way to express yourself in a way that makes you feel good. Write poetry. Write a story. Write a song.

Join a musical group. Take advantage of the opportunities that are around you. If you like math or puzzles, or using your mind with numbers, do that. Think out of the box and ask yourself what you did when you were outside and try to use those same gifts and skills.

True, you don't have access to all the materials or opportunities at hand to do everything you did outside, exactly in the same ways. You can't do what you did to use those skill sets out there, but you can be flexible, creative, and find a way to use what you have now while you are in prison. This may be all like living in prison one to one for you, if you have been there a while, but if you haven't, I hope these suggestions help you. Creativity is a lifeline. It will restore your soul. You have something important to give; your own unique contribution to make, so write to me and send me your brand-new poem.

Hey there, my fellow family and friends, I know you may feel even more shell shocked than your loved-one, if that is even possible. And my comparisons aren't really fair or accurate. I am just trying to illustrate a point. You may feel so helpless and disempowered and sick from it all, as I have, that you can't even dream of getting out of bed. No one is forcing you to, but then again, you probably have other kids at home, a husband, a wife, an older parent to take care of,or a job to go to, so you have no real choice in the matter, even though you may feel like just checking out.

Remember what I said: just breathe. Find something to do with your hands and be creative. You too, can draw, write, sing, play a musical instrument, cook your favorite recipe,etc. What do you like to do? Get out and do it. You may feel guilty at first, as did I. I simply couldn't think of living. Every time I ate a cucumber, since Damien hasn't had fresh vegetablesin 28 years, for example, or whenever I'd go out for a wonderful walk in the park on a nice sunny day, I'd feel guilty, sick, overcome with grief. But, believe me, my dear friends, you have to do these things for yourself. You have got to go outside, look at the flowers, go home and put them in a vase for yourself and enjoy them. You can press them and make pictures like I did. Justdo whatever you can to nourish your soul.

Do what you can do to find something to lift your heart up, so when your loved one calls from prison, in great need and distress, you have something to give. Do all the things you need to, so you can help yourself and him or her fight the good fight of faith. Trust; go slow.
My final little nugget of hope to everyone inside and out, if you take my simple suggestions, persevere, one step, one breath, trust, one day at a time, and in time and eternity, you will prevail.

Chapter Five
Thank You: For What?

(The Importance of Gratitude)

You might say: well, here I am, in this hell hole, and I don't belong here. What is there to be thankful for? Well, remember what I said. You have to get up and decide, yes, decide to live. If you haven't decided to find a way to live, nothing I will say in this book will make any sense, and you will throw it against the wall or even in the trash.

So, I am assuming, that since you are still reading this, you have decided to live, and so, in order to do that, you have to become a master at gratitude. Just look around. Can you walk? Can you stand on your own two feet? If you cannot, or if you happen to be blind or in a wheelchair while in prison wrongly convicted, or a family member, just be thankful for what you can do. Don't focus on what you don't have, but on what you do have. Just make a game of it and go through the entire day thanking God for every little thing, from the moment you get up, till the moment you go to sleep.

I can guarantee that you will be exhausted from it by breakfast time, if you are in prison, and if you are not, your mind will start to wander before you are making peanut butter sandwiches for your kids.

So go ahead, I challenge you: start writing down your gratitude list. It will give you something to do, and it will change your perspective.

You will see that from morning to night,we are showered down upon, as human beings, living on this planet. It's really true that someone is watching over all of us.

You might say, as you are reading this: "This is the worst day of my life! They just denied my appeal for the fifth time" or you may say, "The person in the cell next to me or in my cell with me is a raving lunatic". There is nothing around me except stench, hell, and death. How does anyone give thanks when everything is pure hell, no light, no love, no hope?

Well, as I write this, on this very day, Damien has received his sixth denial. The casewent all the way to the Supreme Court of another state, and it was denied there too. It was deniedon all the issues we have worked on for the past seven years, and yet, we are still giving thanks.

Giving thanks! You might say. What, are you crazy? Well, here's the thing, when you have been close to death, your body disintegrating, your mind totally blown apart by stress, and your nerves just broken to bits so that you can't talk, think, move, hope, or do anything for years on end, eventually, you either just die altogether, and get it over with, or you are resurrected. Yeah, yeah, yeah, you may say. That's you, Lindy, with all your religious stuff again. Well, don't knock it until you try it. You don't have anything to lose, do you?

Chapter Six
Praying in a Foxhole

(Spiritual Practice)

So, on to my next topic. Perhaps you are a person in prison, or a family member, and you don't believe in anything. You don't believe in goodness. You don't have any hope. You don't believe in yourself, and you feel like a total failure. Maybe you feel that way, but as I have said several times, in this writing, and yes, I'll be a broken record and say it again: you have two choices: you either rot away in prison, or at home in your bed like I almost did (but I'll be sure I'm never letting that happen), or, you can decide to thrive, live and spit in the face of the system, while fighting, winning your case and living a good meaningful life.

"How!" You want to scream. Well, like I said, you've got to decide, and decide over and over and over, especially when all those negative horrible pictures and thoughts come pouring into your mind, and believe me, they feel bigger than life, like they are going to swallow you up.

The scariest picture I ever had was: Damien will never get out. He'll just die there, and I won't get to say goodbye. I thought we'd never get to work for God together, or help others, and my life would be a total waste, and all the people who told me what a foolish thing I was doing will have been right, because he was just a waste of my energy all along. Who even cares if you spent the better part of your whole life helping an innocent person? No one will ever know that that person is innocent, because, in the end, they are dead, brought home to you in a body bag, a nameless criminal in the public eye that no one cares anything about, and you just wasted your life on nothing.

Oh, yes, these thoughts, pictures, and feelings. Pictures of Damien coming home in abody bag. Me just burying him with no success for all our hard work. Never being together. No happy days in the sunshine, or even in the rain, (heck) who cares. No vindication for him. No wondrous day of him leaving the courthouse or prison among all his supporters and cheerers-on, like others have had. No such day for us. Just nothing but wasted time, love, blood and tears.

But no! I dared to believe. I dare to believe in the God of my true understanding and conviction, who is Jesus Christ, my Lord, Redeemer, Savior, and everlasting God. And I must tell you, I am not disappointed, even though he has gotten five denials, because I have given my will and my entire being to God. I just look at God, and let everything else go.

Whatever God thinks is best. Even if one of us dies before this is over, the other will carry on and glorify God. No matter what happens, together or apart, we will keep on fighting forthe justice for all people. We will keep on helping people and give them solace in every way possible.

So, you see, my friend, whoever you are reading this book, whether inside, in a lonely prison cell, or outside; a wife, mother, brother, friend, girlfriend, niece, nephew, or a lawyer who cares about your client, you can't lose if you put everything in God's hands and trust in the goodness and mercy of God.

You have to look up, not down, forward, not back, ahead, not behind. You have to keep saying thank you. Keep thinking about success and keep finding a way to connect with a deeper more eternal reality than yourself, and what you can see with your physical eyes. Everything passes. This prison thing will pass. I didn't think so, but it will. I was so hurt, thinking yeah, it will pass when one of us dies. What satisfaction will we have, never having gotten anywhere? You have to completely let go, and let God take over your life. Because right now, you are chained by the way you think.

You must just pray for one thing: God's will. Life is short. Use every moment to love andto spread love. I know you may think I am crazy, but if I let my eyes and heart just be down here on this earth, I would have drowned in despair.

Please, find a relationship with God. Pray and turn to God. Open your heart. Give God your heart. Pray for peace in your heart. Make a daily practice of prayer. Practice loving God first and foremost and loving those who are around you. If you make this your highest purpose inevery moment, you will have plenty to focus on, and plenty that will give meaning to your life.

So you may ask, "How will you make it through yet another denial?" I will not only make it, but Damien and I will soar higher and higher, doing God's will, embracing God's will, living in God's will, and drowning in God's will. In that way, we will be supremely happy, living a life of purposeful love, and rejoicing that God is using us in these circumstances. After all, someone must curse the darkness with a candle

Special prayer

Jesus, my Lord and God, You who walked this earth as a real human being, but yet who never lost your total divinity, I pray to You, who are here with me now. I open my heart completely, without reserve to You. I leave everything in Your blessed hands.

I trust You.

I believe in You.

I believe You love me, and know what my heart needs to live.

It isn't Your will that I or my loved one go down to the dust to disintegrate in disgrace, ordespair, so I trust You to do what it is good, right, just, and to do the very best thing that will bring as many souls comfort and happiness, freedom, joy and everlasting love and life, and I trust You completely with this injustice. You see everything, and if there has been another delay, You are in charge, and know all about it, and You will see that it works together for our goodand for the good of all men and women. So I thank You and praise You, and keep my eyes on You with complete confidence at all times.

Breathe in thanksgiving and trust. Breathe out thanksgiving and trust. Rejoice in hope, faith and love. Amen, alleluia!

Chapter Seven
How Can I Go On?

(How to Make it Through Hard Days)

Well, I'm sure by now, you can imagine, I have had my share of hard days! I started to analyze things, and ask myself: why is this day so hard? Unresolved trauma was making it hardto get through the day. Carrying pain from the past was weighing me down.

The definition of trauma is an event that overwhelms a person's nervous system. Theperson is simply not able to cope, to process a certain event or events, not even physically.Traumas are terrible shocks to the system, like when soldiers come back from war shell-shocked.

Well, news flash, we are all in a war, a vast and terrible war with the corruption of the justice system. The system has made horrific, evil errors, and that is why we got into this situation in the first place. But we must also realize that we are in a spiritual battle.

Evil really does exist. You may wonder about that, but it does. If you are reading this, andyou aren't a professing Christian, I encourage you to open your heart to the possibility of true love, such that true love exists only in the love of Jesus, who is God. You don't have to accept organized religion if you have been turned off by it, but just open your heart and do your best to open it simply, like a hungry child opens its mouth to the mother, who feeds him or her.

So, we are in a spiritual battle. It is a battle for your soul. It is a battle for my soul. We have weapons we can use to fight this battle. Besides being on top of your game, taking care of yourself emotionally, since you are in this dire situation, you must have a spiritual belief of somekind. You must dedicate yourself to thriving, not to dying. It is your choice. Evil forces would like nothing better than for you to give up and despair. Here's how evil forces tempt you:

They put pictures in your mind, scary pictures, painful pictures, despairing pictures. You may have dark and negative thoughts, and empty agonizing thoughts, like: "No one cares about me. I will die in this prison," or, "My husband, wife, sister, brother, or friend will die in there…"

Listen, I believe there is a real devil, and the devil wants to destroy you. The devil will use things like terrible pictures to get you down, off track and sinking. Some of the terrible, despairing pictures that evil used get me to sink: Damien will collapse in his cell. He will die there. You will never say goodbye. You will never see him again. Your life is worth nothing.

These were especially painful and horrific for me, because I had felt alone most of mylife and had believed that God sent me to Damien, and Damien to me, for a divine purpose. If I didn't get to say goodbye and he died in prison alone, everything we had worked for would be a total waste and a sham. All that I had hoped for my entire life, in my desires to serve God, wouldnever be realized. I would be empty. It would be like my life was worthless. Everyone would think Damien is a criminal or murderer. This hurt badly.

What I had to do was learn to fight these thoughts. Family members are very fortunate, because we can go to various types of trauma healing therapies which can remove the trauma andthe scary agonizing pictures and sensations from a person's body and mind. Such therapies, as EMDR, biofeedback, neurofeedback, ACT and somatic therapies, can take the stress of traumaticimages and pictures away.

I know, my dear friend in prison, that you don't have access to these things, but in time, I hope to be able to develop a long-distance therapy that can help you heal from the stress of trauma that you feel. It doesn't matter if you are not here in person, but you must be kind to yourself.

Remember that scary pictures and negative thoughts are just that. It is like a movie screenin your mind, and a script that plays over and over, but you don't have to listen. You MUST reprogram your mind. You must become aware of what you think and choose to only nourishand feed thoughts that will help you remain strong, even in prison. There are examples of people who have done this, even on death row.

Another thing that would get me tripped up, and feeling very sick inside, sick at heart,and filled with grief was realizing that Damien couldn't sit out on the porch with me in the summertime, or go for a walk in the beautiful spring evenings, or go to the beach, and put hisfeet in the ocean, or listen to a beautiful song on the radio with me.

When holidays would come around, all the rest of my family would be sitting around the table. In my heart and mind, I repeatedly would feel the stabbing pain of an absence, of a separation. Likewise, there is no guarantee it will get resolved while we are both on earth, but, until my last breath, I will fight for and beside Damien, and as I fight for Damien I will keep fighting for others.

You must have strong faith, hope, love. Thirst, all the more, for faith, hope and love. Otherwise, you will sink down in despair. How about doing what I have learned to do instead, when I turned one of these very sad pictures and days into a happy one? On Memorial Day, recently, I was sad that he couldn't be home. I said to myself, this is what I'll do. I'm going to change things around. This will work. Instead of him being home here, drinking lemonade on my sister's nice back porch, I imagined we were drinking from a beautiful, golden cup, the divine cup of nectar: faith, hope and love. How sweet the nectar was! We were lifted above the Earth. Sadness and misery faded away into eternal joy. I just keep turning my eyes to heaven in realizing a purposeful joy.

Whatever meaning you can give to your situation, please do it, and lift your eyes andheart upward to a heavenly reality, to goodness that resides deep inside you, and far beyond any prison walls. Remember that the Gospel says: "Blessed are the poor in spirit, for theirs is the kingdom of God...." I think what that means is: the more helpless you are, and the more you throw yourself completely on the mercy of God, with complete abandon, the happier you will be. Then, the Lord will smile down upon you and give you peace.

So, my dear friend and traveler over these troubled seas, remember; you have a Master who has gone before you. Any suffering you can name, Jesus has undergone it. Loneliness,yes. Betrayal, yes. Abandonment, yes. People falsely accusing him, yes. Misunderstanding and false judgment, yes. Humiliation, yes. Degradation, yes. Physical brutality, yes. What has He not gone through, that you are undergoing now? And, my dear fellow friend and family member of the beloved wrongly convicted, you are like Mary, the holy and blessed mother, who stood byher Son, helpless, and shattered, but yet fully confident in the goodness and mercy of God.

Let us imitate the Lord and Our Lady and let us rejoice that we have an opportunity to carry thiscross, so that we may rise to a higher plane of virtue, joy and love.

Amen.

Chapter Eight
Just Hang On
(How To Fight Despair)

Lest I say all the same things over and over, and you get frustrated or bored, and think I just don't understand, let me tell you I know that despair is a powerful force. It can paralyzeyou. I am going to say right from the start that hope is a true gift. You must pray for it. You mustlook for it.

Once in my life, before this started, I was feeling overcome by despair. One of my friendspicked me a small bouquet of wildflowers, and I put them in a bud vase on my dresser. I touched those flowers several times a day to remind myself that there was still hope. Put tangible signs around you to remind yourself there is hope, because there still is. We are all here for a divine plan. Once you get past the bitterness and shock, which may recur, you have to realize you are here for a higher purpose.

I look to Jesus on the cross and to the lives of heroic people, such as Clara Barton, HarrietTubman, Abraham Lincoln, and the Christian Saints. I have made it my life's purpose to imitate Jesus and to let my will be turned over to God's.

So, I am no longer attaching myself to the outcomes of this situation. For so many years, my hope was based on whether Damien would get out or not. I simply saw in my heart's and mind's eye, that if

45

he stayed there for life, my own life's purpose would be so significantly affected, that it would be ruined as well. It would be thwarted by the prison system also. I believed this because I thought we had a joint life purpose in serving God.

I also made this same crucial mistake earlier in my life, when I thought that if I couldn't become a nun, or that if such and such a thing didn't happen, my life's purpose wouldn't be completed, but that is simply not true. I am still having a good, thriving hope-filled life, even though Damien isn't home yet, and I have no idea when or even "if" for certain, he will get here, before our time is up on earth.

My own dreams of living a life totally given to God have been fulfilled. I am living the life I have always wanted because I am living as a Catholic Carmelite hermit with religious vows. I am happy! I see now that God can work out his plan in whatever way he wishes and God is not dependent on external Earthbound realities.

There is most certainly a time when I couldn't dare to write those words, or even say them, because it hurt too much. I have turned my will and life over to God, and I trust with all my heart and soul that God is working out a good plan. It doesn't have to be my plan or Damien's, and in fact I beg God that it will not be. I have said since the beginning that if Damiennever came home, I would accept it.

Love is strong. We have freedom of choice, and I choose to put all my hope in God.

I am no longer attached to the outcome of this situation, and I have decided to thrive. If you are on the outside, listen to YouTube videos that

46

can help you boost your faith and hope. Get help from a trained and competent therapist, or someone who truly understands tragedy. Believe me,it will help you fight despair if you move forward. The more you stay stuck, the worse you will feel. You have to realize it is okay to move forward.

That might sound strange, but I felt guilty if I moved forward in my life and Damien just stayed in prison. It will be unfair, but, everyone has to make a life where they are. Once, Damientold me: "You know, people build lives in here, and we are all right." I almost punched him. I was so mad, but still...

A couple years ago, it dawned on me, that I had been consumed with this. As much as I love Damien, I realized that maybe, just maybe, I could move forward and rebuild my life. It wasokay to start writing, singing, dancing, going for walks, and enjoying my life. It dawned on me, actually, that my life is separate than Damien's.

He has his journey. I have mine. I can't live his life for him, no matter how much I want him to be out of prison. He can't live mine for me. We each are responsible for the quality of ourown life. I can't take his sufferings away, as much as I would like to, and he can't take mine away either. We must realize that acceptance is an active word. If you are in prison, and you just feel overcome, pray to be able to breathe, and stay in this moment only. Yes, you are living in a hellish situation, to put it mildly, and certainly I don't want to underestimate it! But, deep inside, you must realize your body is there; your mind and spirit do not have to be there.

Look up. Look forward. Make something beautiful for yourself to look at. I would feel somuch panic, despair, pain, and sickness in my mind and body, that I would just put on some Christian music, and sing as loud as I could. There are certain skills you can learn to help to soothe yourself and to tolerate distress. I didn't know any of these things.

Be kind to yourself. Go outside, and feel the grass, or look up at the sky. Drink it in and feel the coolness on your face. Let what is available to you, help you. Pray for the grace to open your eyes and heart. God is all around you. You are in God's presence. Remember there is no one who suffered more than Jesus the Lord and Master. He suffered abandonment, despair, but only as a human being. He felt that He too was at the end of the road. Remember, he was basically on death row, and was executed as an innocent man.

Do everything you do for Him, because if you are in that position, you are a martyr for the system, and you are sacrificing your life for a higher purpose, to stand as a testimony to the whole world, that the system needs to be changed. Without people being willing to sacrifice theirlives, nothing will ever change. Think about the great changes that have happened in history. In order for slavery to be abolished, many slaves were tortured and killed, and the change came at a very high price. Yet, the deep problem of hatred, racism, and prejudice is not eradicated.

We must continue to fight. You must realize that your life, no matter how tortured you have been, or are being, in mind, body, or spirit…that you are fulfilling a very holy and high purpose. This message will not be received by everyone, but if you are open and generous enough, and if you want to find true salvation, in the literal and best sense of the word, you must humbly oblige yourself to accept this.

The cross of Christ was an instrument of torture and death in ancient times. It was the electric chair of those days. Embrace where you are and open your heart. Be an instrument of peace to the men and women around you. If you love someone with a double life sentence as I do, or if you love an innocent man or woman on death row, remember Mary, the Mother of God, was in your position. I have asked myself many times: how did she do it? She realized that she too, was carrying in unison with her Divine Son, the cross, and being executed in her heart.

Let it be for a higher purpose. You too are suffering the casualty of the system's heinous crimes. But, it is not for naught. Lift your heart to the Lord and give Him thanks.

Chapter Nine

Every Day is Christmas,

Thanksgiving andEaster

(How to Make it Through The Holidays)

That dreaded time, holidays! How can I make it through, you may ask? You could sleep, and just let the whole day go by. You could think: Well, holidays don't mean anything, since I am in prison, or why celebrate because my dear loved one isn't here, but really, how would that help?

Holidays in prison are a nothing time. A more than excruciating time. More suicides and fights happen then. More and more horrific things. People are lonelier than ever. They are sad. Trapped. Outside, how many holidays did I spend with my heart in my throat, or with my heart deep down in despair? Yes, that thing I just told you about beating, with all the wonderful wisdom I have gained in this wilderness. How, you ask, do you make it?

Well, every holiday, probably just like you, I hurt. Damien not here beside me at the holiday dinner table, not holding his hand when we gathered to pray, but someone else's. Not sharing Christmas, Thanksgiving, or Easter with him. Knowing that he had no special meal,

50

but pressed turkey from a can or box, with salty processed instant potatoes, not to mention no good vegetables. (A horror to my health-conscious vegetarian mind). Yeah, I know the meal is awful. But people are starving in Bangladesh. Didn't you ever hear the old saying of eat your vegetables because kids are starving in Africa?

What are holidays anyway? A time to spend with loved ones and family? A time to celebrate great spiritual truths, and to rejoice? I simply couldn't celebrate when my friend was six hundred miles away in a prison, wrongfully! I dreaded holidays.

I remember the first or second Thanksgiving here without Damien. I was cooking Thanksgiving dinner for all our Lighthouse guests, peeling lots of sweet potatoes the day before.I remember getting ready on Wednesday, when everyone all over America was getting their stuffing and turkey dinners prepped. I was miserable. I couldn't think of anything to celebrate, soI just pushed myself through, making this massive meal for I don't know what.

Every holiday was like that. I'd put up a tree, and send Damien pictures, but it just wasn'tthe same. Why did it hurt so badly? I just couldn't accept that he was there, yet, another holiday, and let alone, a day or another year, wrongfully!!! "When is this ever going to end?" My twin sister asks, after yet another Christmas had passed.

After a while you just lose count. You don't remember quite how many years, or do you? Well, if you are like me, you remember everything, every single detail of everything. In some ways, it turns into a thick blur in your mind. In any case, this holiday thing has got to be mastered, or it will kill you.

Well, what I discovered is this. Here is my magical secret! Every holiday, yes, every day,in fact, is a reason to celebrate. All the things I treasured and held so dearly, like opening Christmas presents together, sitting by a cozy tree, eating Thanksgiving dinner, singing carols, baking, or being with family, all the little things that mean so much…yes, yes, indeed they are to cherished and they are missed, make no mistake about that. (I am not going to write a Pollyanna fake story) But truly, all those things are earthly things. They are passing, and they are temporary. They aren't actually what the holidays are about.

Christmas is about the birth of Jesus; About his coming into this world; our light, ourhope, our salvation. That is something no prison or wrongful conviction can obliterate, no matterhow thick the walls are, and no matter how foreboding the two life sentences may feel and seem. The operative word here is "seem", because yes, they feel dreadful, but like I said before, thecross is to be embraced, not avoided.

We are Christians, remember, and even if you are reading this and you are not, there is a purpose for all suffering if embraced and accepted with a childlike trusting heart. Remember those words of Jesus in the Gospel when He says: "Whoever can accept this, do so. Whoever hasears to hear, let him hear"? Not all do. Not all will, but if you are reading this, maybe, please God, you do.

Christmas cannot be destroyed just because we don't open Christmas presents together or decorate the tree. For Christians, springtime comes, and Easter comes. Now for sure, it isn't about chocolate bunnies and stuff like that. I always felt extremely sad when springtime came, like yet, another year, and my melancholy self, all Irish, Italian, and Native American full of emotions and yearnings, would hurt badly, and just ache.

As Christians, we believe in the resurrection of Jesus and in new beginnings. We believe that all evil has and will be conquered by Christ; that hell, death, and destructive evil of false imprisonment will be forever conquered. As I grow older and wiser, I see that my life wasn't a waste after all. I can rejoice.

No prison can take away Easter and the power of the Resurrection. Even if we don't get what we want, in the end we will always get what we need. If I want to rejoice, I can! No one can take my joy away from me, because it isn't based on any source here, but in the God who is risen from the dead. My treasure is in heaven.

Thanksgiving cannot be ruined because we don't bake pumpkin pies together, or sit around watching football, no matter how precious sitting around a family table with loved ones surely is. Every day is Thanksgiving, and every day Damien and I give thanks, because no prison sentence and no two natural life sentences can take away our gratitude to God.

And here is the last thought I want to leave you with regarding holidays: Holidays and celebrations point to realities and things that are divine. They remind us of divine love, everlasting joy, and happiness. That is what heaven is and will be like. We all long for heaven, whether

53

we realize it or not. We all want love that doesn't fade or leave us alone. We all want peace in our hearts. That is what we can have, if only we open our hearts. That is how we find heaven's key.

In the old days, my friend reading this, when I was just doing prison ministry, I used to purposely spend holidays with the people at my local county jail. "Why?", you might ask incredulously. But being with my friends there helped me cope through difficult times. Yeah, thepeople there really helped me. The people there were funny. They had a blast on Thanksgiving. They had a crazy whipped cream fight. "Get out of the way! Watch out Lindy!" a woman shouted as scoops of fluffy white clouds were hurled, hitting me in the face. They found something to do and a reason to laugh. Yeah, they got away with that in the county jail.

So, once again I am telling you, you must never lose hope. On holidays, you must find something to celebrate! You must look up toward heaven, and give thanks for the life you have, and think about what the true meaning of this holiday is. Use your gratitude skills, and count all your blessings, even if your life seems like it is a mess.

If it is your birthday, and no one has sent you a card, make one for yourself. If it is Easter,or Passover, or another holiday, find a creative way of celebrating. You can write a poem, draw apicture, make cards for people to or just train yourself to celebrate the little things. The reason for this is that celebrating, not only holidays, but something to be grateful about every day, will make your time in prison easier and much more pleasant. If you are a family member or friend, pining away for your loved one, like I did the first seven years of this adventure, just love them with all your heart, and believe in the power of love.

Holidays were given to us to celebrate. Even though you are going this through this terrible grief and feeling of helplessness, realize that if you are standing by your loved one in whatever capacity you can, you are doing a very heroic thing. The suffering you have is hidden from everyone else. No one believes in the innocence of your loved one except you, or hardly anyone anyway, so use this holiday to be especially good to yourself, so you can keep standing by your loved one with support, hope and faith.

Do something nice for yourself. When you eat an ice cream, or your favorite dessert, eat half for your loved one. Do it deliberately and mindfully. Plan ways to share good things, such aswriting a holiday story together, or doing a special project together through the mail, even if it is something you have never done before. The point is, you have to be creative, and do what will truly benefit you and your loved one, and being overcome with grief will not help you.

When the feelings of grief come, do not fight them. Feel them. Write about them and let them pass. Celebrate that you are together as mother and son or whatever you may be, and that you have had the fortitude to keep your bond strong. Celebrate that your loved one is still fighting, and stand by him or her, realizing that you and your wrongfully convicted loved one areheroes.

You are meant to fight, and you have a purpose and a mission that will not only help you but will help so many other people who are also trapped by the injustices of the system.

Do whatever it takes to decide (yes, there's that word again) to be happy during this day, and thismoment only, and if you turn the corners of your mouth into even the slightest smile, instead of that downcast frown, you will amazingly see that it is starting to help you feel better. Every dayis a gift. We must make it count.

Amen.

Chapter Ten
On This Rock

(How to Strengthen Your Faith)

Well, day by day, day by day. Yeah, yeah, yeah I know, but they days are awful and monotonous; all that day by day, drudgery bologna. Just the same old waiting in line for the umpteenth time, out in the cold for the phone, or whatever, and so much chaos all around.

What's good about this day anyway? Same day same thing. Nothing good. What do you think? Well, I just want you to know, that we, on the outside, feel the same way at times. That is the temptation that we all face, of letting our minds gravitate and wander toward the dark and negative side of things. Our minds will just do that sometimes. Our minds are the battleground. We can't make negative thoughts go away by forcing them down and pushing them away.

They will just come back with a vengeance, like if you push a spring down with all your might; well, wonder of wonders, lo and behold, it just pops back up again. All that physical and mental exertion did nothing, no good at all!

So, how do you get rid of the blues on a cold snowy day in the middle of a winter inNorth Dakota, or on a blazing hot, 110-degree day in Arizona or Texas? I'm telling you, take it from me. You can't will the blues and boredom away. You just have to be present to whatever is going on inside you, and outside your control, and let it be. If a negative thought comes up and says: "I ain't doing a damn thing with my life; all this trying is getting me nowhere," well, just acknowledge it. Say out loud, or under your breath, so the person around you doesn't think you're too crazy. Just say: "Oh, yeah, I see you, scary awful picture; I hear you; negative accusatory thought."

Thoughts are just like that; They are like annoying pesky flies. They come and go, and they might keep coming back. You just need to let them be. Even when your body feels like it is in an eternal freezer or hot as hell, or your mind just feels like it is trapped in an endless circle of tormenting thoughts, or your heart feels like someone is squeezing it to death, just be. Just be in this moment! I can't stress this enough. Don't run away; don't fight with what is.

My simple answer? My simple salve for all wounds? Look at the cross! Look at Jesus! He is hanging there, naked, beaten bludgeoned to death, burning up by the endless violence and hatred of all mankind from beginning of time till now; freezing to end less death by the coldness of all our hearts.

Does He not notice? Does He not feel? Does He not have compassion on your poor suffering, anguished, miserable soul? He does! Just look at Him continually, and in His face and eyes, and heart, you will find all you are looking for. You will find strength for this moment, this day, this week, this month, this year, this decade and this life. Alleluia!

Chapter Eleven
You Are One of a Kind

(How to Find Purpose)

So, my dear friend, we only have a couple more chapters to go in this little book, which I have written from my heart to yours. And now that we are practicing, practicing, practicing, and maybe haven't got it quite mastered yet, but we are working on it; yes, we are! What do you do to find purpose? How can there be any purpose to a life in a five by seven cell, with nothing to do, but scratch a couple of things on line paper, or in staring at the same old television programs? How can there be any purpose in all the running around I am doing, trying to keep my loved one going? There is always endless frustration and discouragement trying to get me off track. How do I beat it and find purpose?

> Well, every day, get up! Get up, look up! Look up, not down. Look forward, not back.

The past is truly taken care of by God; all those bad memories that flash into your mind, and make you feel paralyzed, stultified; they really are under the blood of Jesus, cleansed by Him, understood by Him! They are, because when you ask Him to do so for you, He will and He does. He knows how lonely September felt, when it seemed everyone on the outside of prison was going on with their life for yet another school year, while here you sit (so-called) rotting away.

Come on now, friends on the outside, we have our version of it too. We want to be with you! We miss you! Oh, how we miss you!! Life isn't really worth anything living without you, isit? How can we find purpose when you are there? But we have to or we die. We have to or we will rot out here too; makes no difference whether a person is confined in a prison of steel and bars, or a prison of despair within one's soul. Does it?

We can move around and eat something good when we want to, and I am not saying that all that doesn't matter. Just how beautiful and blissful such freedoms are, and you are probably thinking, yeah, how good a steak, a nice juicy steak, or a hot fudge sundae would taste right now.But, I have tell you, I'm vegetarian, and pretty weird; so I don't dream about juicy steak hot off the grill, but whatever your fancy, yes, we have those external freedoms, and you might think it makes life better, and it does in a way, but we have the oppression of prison on the other side of the wall.

Have you ever thought about that? We are bearing the flip side of what you are bearing, we who love you. You are there, in that confined space, doing the same thing every day, and paying for something you didn't do. We have a truckload of responsibilities out here: a job, house, kids, finances, traveling back and forth to see you, and paying for the expenses you may have (and you know how expensive everything is in prison). It is a wonder that we can even do all that. Each of us has our share of the hardship, because this dreadful wrongful conviction doesn't just affect you; it affects every single person who loves you and is trying to stand by you.

You have the slow, painful days of being there, but you have to make it work, or die, as you have discovered, just by sure necessity. We have the slow, endless nights of missing you and of trying not to go crazy or die of a heart attack. We are trying to cope with the never-ending stress of keeping all fires burning on all fronts, just to keep this fight going.

So, we are both carrying this cross together, and we must hang tough. How do we keep meaning and purpose and how do we find it in this uphill climb? My answer is, of course, to look at Jesus. Look at the fact that heaven exists. You might not think it does, but it does. We are living in this world for a heavenly reality, not an earthly one. If you thought your purpose was thriving at a job, or making money, or having what you want in your life and doing what you want on the weekends, think again.

Why are you here anyway? Why am I? Why is anyone anywhere, in any terrible or seemingly dreadful situation? Is God cruel, or is God kind? Did the people who suffered and died in concentration camps just die for no purpose? Or did they have a purpose, even though no one knew their names? They were numbers on a prison roster. Six million of them. They weren't identified to anyone as they died horrendous deaths. What's the sense in that? Has God forsaken us? What's the sense of a nameless life dying alone or rotting away in prison? What's the sense of the quiet, killing despair we have, outside those concrete walls, as we pine away for you, with no control over what may or may not happen?

The answer is Jesus. Jesus. Jesus! Look at Him! I am shouting this to you! Pleading this to you! Our purpose is not earthly. Our purpose is to live out this wrongful conviction thing in God's way, in God's arms, in God's economy. Please do this. Look for Him. Talk to Him. Let Him into your life, so He can tell you all the answers you seek and why you are in that prison. Why, o precious loved one, why you are grieving your life away? You mustn't! That's right! You must not! Yes, you are grieving, but you must unite your grief to Jesus and that of His mother who stood by the cross!

You in prison, you are like a bright light shining in the darkness of hell for all your brothers and sisters who surround you. Open up. Be what you are meant to be, right where you are. No excuses. It is your choice and mine. When you feel you can't go on, remember, there is someone on the other side of this page who knows exactly what you feel. I wouldn't be writing this if I didn't, so let's press on together, and do whatever we do each day for God and for the sake of eternal love and everlasting life. Amen.

Chapter Twelve
Hope Springs Eternal
(How to Keep Hope Alive)

A huge question, right? I have had bad days; very bad, when I just felt paralyzed by grief,but yet, another thing going wrong; and indeed, the little things can really get you down! Since I am blind and have been working on the case of Damien for many years, things are hard, very hard. For instance, when I send an email, I have to use a screen reader and if something goes wrong with it, there might not be any way I can get anything done, because sighted people use technology differently. To do small things, such looking up an address or something online, is very difficult and is at least five extra steps that are too complicated to explain. Life can be very tedious and endlessly exhausting, since I have a serious illness that causes me to feel the effects of stress severely. My body can feel sick after the smallest amount of exertion. It is like I am carrying five tons of weight on my back, and I can't think, walk, sleep, eat, and I feel very sick atthe tiniest mention of anything painful or stressful. I am trying to labor to climb up this hill of fighting a wrongful conviction, when my body doesn't feel good a lot of the time.

Things at the prison are painful and used to practically destroy me. Damien would call and say that they aren't giving him the proper insulin or that some of his medications were taken away arbitrarily. He would call and say he had another denial in the case, or three books which I had to pay top dollar for have been returned because of some small glitch or some mistake that was made when they were ordered. When Damien calls and says the phones are outside, and it is ten below zero, I feel it in my bones. When we tried to call a lawyer's office for the fifth monthin a row, trying to get one simple answer, it was very tiring-- the list goes on and on.

Damien is very balanced and equanimous. He has a joyful spirit. How on earth has he developed this quality? I don't know. He told me that many years ago, he developed the practice,a conscious deliberate practice of inviting the presence of God to come and be with him in the moment he is in, and he consciously puts himself in God's presence and focuses only on what hecan do in this moment, with gratitude and love. A lot of this book has been about an attitude change, or a perspective change, but it is more than that; much more. It is about opening to the grace of God. It is about accepting life as it is and embracing the cross and God's will.

Once, a few years ago, I went to see a very holy prayerful nun, who told me what I reallyneeded to know. I thought I would go there and hear some profound wisdom that would makemy whole task easier and ease all my pain and sorrow, but she only said one very disappointing thing: "Embrace God's will." At the time, I thought that was a rather generic bland thing to say, and plus, God's will was quite devastating and disappointing to me anyway. What was God's will anyway? Was it always meant to destroy us and break us down, like the old scenarios I used to hear people talk about? Well, if I embrace God's will, or pray for just that alone, maybe God will most assuredly make me do the thing I hate. Maybe He will make me lose my kids, go to Africa to be a missionary, or get cancer, or something awful that will destroy me. Those thoughtsjust makes me feel depressed, praying for God's will, and they don't give me any hope. But,what really, is God's will? I was always afraid to pray for it too, even though I did pray. I prayed and prayed for it, during this period of my life and for my whole life, but I was always afraid. My life had been rather disappointing up until this period, and I just had no idea what Godwas up to, but little by little, I kept praying and praying for God's will. It was something like the Old Testament story of putting "your Isaac on the altar" and keeping it there. Giving God the most important thing in your heart, and letting God be God.

First, I prayed desperately for Damien's freedom. It was like I was living and dying on it, terrified whenever I didn't hear from him at the appointed time, having all kinds of terrible tortuous pictures in my mind and heart, like maybe he had been killed in prison and was dead on the floor of his cell. Maybe he had been violently killed or beaten by the guards, or maybe I would never see him again. Oh, how such pictures and feelings tortured me!

I remember the first time he didn't call when I thought he was going to. I was beside myself and remained in this state for several years in my heart; fighting the case, and doing all that was required. I was doing all the leg work like raising money for lawyers, doing legal research, etc., and I had no idea what I was doing! It was scary, hard and painful every day. It was a terrible fight. I had my whole life wrapped up in what would happen in the case. I didn't think I could live if it never got resolved. I just truly didn't think so, because I had waited all my life to live in fellowship with someone who was of like mind; spiritually I just thought, if he never gets out of prison, there will be no hope for my life. I will die, not ever having completed what God wanted of me. We just will end up fighting this evil system, and our lives will be a complete failure. This type of dreadful, emotional pain and heartbreak wore me down.

"But you can't go down with the ship," I have heard some people say. Plus, I had given my life, and I wasn't going to stop now. When I was at the height of physical sickness, the doctors said, "You will have some very bad days". For a long time, I just wondered what was going to happen to my life. I really didn't know if I was going to make it. I just knew I lovedGod and couldn't give up. All this was going on during the worst of the pandemic. Damien would call and tell me treacherously bad news. "The whole prison is on quarantine. Everyone is sick. People are dying around me," he said. I just had to keep on putting my life in God'shands. It is easy to say, but hard to do. The only thing I can tell you is that there is one thing that mattered more to me than anything else, and that was and is God. I always wanted to serve God first, and love God.

Since I was young, I wanted to be a nun. I love God with my whole heart and that love carried me through. Sometimes I would be so angry and hurt. I had to learn how to deal with my feelings. I had to learn to just accept myself and my feelings as they were. I couldn't make them go away. I had to just realize this was painful and was going to be

66

until or unless it ended. Finally, though there is much more to describe in between, and no way to really describe it, I came to terms with it all. My goal is no longer to get Damien out of prison, but it is indeed,to live in God's will, not just to embrace God's will, but to live in it, and to immerse myself init. That certainly doesn't mean we are going to stop fighting for justice in Damien's case, however. Nor does it mean that God puts his stamp of approval on wrongful convictions! We aregoing to keep fighting and I am going to keep fighting for every single person that crosses my path. I am going to keep helping every friend and family member that contacts me.

Be that as it may, for me, living in God's will is the dream of a lifetime. I prayed, when I was young, that I could be totally consumed by Divine love and spread it around to everyone, and that is what I will do for the rest of my life. God's will is nothing other than love, true love, that no prison, no wrongful conviction, no hurt, no pain, no tragedy, can take away. God's will ispeace that is deep, real and unchanging, no matter what is going on in our lives.

So, how do you keep hope alive when you are living through this tragedy, or carrying thiscross? You realize that all suffering on earth is in union with Jesus' sufferings on the cross. You put Him in the center of your life and keep on doing so, with every breath, every heartbeat, every step, every word, and every action. You no longer live for yourself and your own dreams, plans, and little ideas and thoughts, but for God alone, and for an eternal purpose. You realize that evil exists, but you are not daunted by it. You look up with gratitude in your heart for every little

67

thing, even for the pain which you realize can produce great gifts of love for others, if only you can open your heart to God's grace working through all things.

Lest this sound like empty preaching, I can only pray that my words will take effect. As I said before, if someone reading this is open, they will hear; if not, they will not. Hope is from God, no other source. The way to keep hope alive and to keep it blazing is to turn away from all other false fleeting sources of hope, such as in what will happen in your case or in wondering about how things go in your future. You may ask yourself, "Will what I want to happen or not?".But to turn only to God, to trust God's great plan and to live only for a divine eternal purpose: that is how hope stays alive. That is how hope flourishes. Amen.

Chapter Thirteen
On Eagle's Wings
(How to Thrive)

"They that wait on the Lord shall renew their strength. They shall run and not be weary. Theyshall walk and not faint." (Isaiah 40, verse 31).

Oh, yes, oh, yes, now at last, we come to the crux of what this book is really about: thriving! How? You may ask, in incredibility. How on earth can a person not just survive, and barely exist in this situation? Now I am going to give you the answer: Listen up! For most of my life, my dear precious reader and friend, I have "just existed..." Yes, I know; I know. That's hardto believe for a person like me, a person who looked like I did so much on the outside. Like I accomplished so much, was so busy, productive and all that blah blah blah. I founded a nonprofitministry to help the poor and needy, and went all over the place singing in prisons, nursing homes, and churches; I spoke in so many churches, and tried to give a home to so many people, whoever would come to my door. I did all this, and yet, and yet, oh, sadness of my heart! I felt like I was just in a boat that was sinking, and I was trying to bail out the water with a thimble. The harder I worked, the more the water of adversity and suffering would come in. The more people's lives were shattered, the more it broke my heart, the harder I worked, and the more overwhelmed

I got.

So, I did a lot, but I was empty. Why? Because I knew I was meant for something greater,something higher, something more sublime. Have you ever felt like your life was passing youby? Like you just weren't really in the right place, or the right situation, like that old saying of being in the right church but the wrong pew? For me, it was much more feeling displaced than being in the right church and in just the wrong pew. It wasn't a case of just moving over a little, for heaven's sake. I just felt more and more tired, more and more sad. Every time Spring would come, I would think about my life as I was growing older, wondering what on earth I was doing. Deep, deep inside, all I wanted to do was love God, truly love God, sing for joy and love of God,and tell the whole world that God exists. I wanted to tell the whole universe that no matter how bad things are in one's life down here, there is a great heaven, and life is much more than what meets the eye, breaks the heart or crushes the soul. I just couldn't get the message out, and my heart felt weighed down by all the suffering I endured and all the pain of others around me.

So, my dear friend and reader, how did I ever come to the place, that for the first time in my life, springtime isn't sad, and as the birds outside begin to sing in early March, my heart doesn't sink, and I no longer think my life is empty? I came to this realization, that one day, today, as a matter of fact, I can smile and I can live. I don't have to be afraid and I can step into my brand new life and just embrace this life with my arms wide open to my future. I can do it without any trepidation or fear, because God is holding me by the hand, and the angels are guarding my tiny little heartbeats. Mary, my mother, and the mother of us all, is guiding me by the hand into living God's will. In the Scriptures, it says that the food of Jesus was to do the will of God; that He had no other food, so for me, now, when I wake up in the morning, it is like I have found my daily bread.

All the things I ached for in the past, as the days, weeks, months, years and decades slipped by—all those things that made me hurt so badly, thinking that everyone had a life except me, everyone had love, everyone had comfort, everyone had beautiful springtime at their fingertips, and I was still waiting to live. I was still waiting for things to work out with my life. I was waiting for things not to hurt and for love to come. But oh, how blind I was, because all this time, God had a plan, and I just didn't know what it was. When I look back, I can see how God provided for me. God sent me friends; God sent me company. God sent me work to do, people tolove and people to love me. Was it perfect? No. Did it take away all the pain? No, but it is like I was walking around in a fog, or almost dead, deadened by grief, sadness, and waiting for something to happen. I had no promises that anything would change. I just knew that God was with me. God would see to it that my life would not just be destroyed by grief or tragedy. However, even though I didn't feel that, deep down, I tried to trust.

You might be reading this thinking: "So, are you saying, don't wait to get out? Don't fight for it? Don't hope? Are you crazy, you crazy stupid woman, you religious nut?" But, no, that isn't what I'm saying. Before you throw this book away, please just listen to two more paragraphs. What I am saying is this. We were put here for a reason. It isn't our plan, nor are youor neither am I in the center of this plan of God, for which we were put here and made. If wehave and are suffering adversity, which we surely are, we are human, and we join the ranks of all suffering people all over the world, especially in our troubled times. The war in Ukraine goes on as write this book. Abused children in middle class America are growing up alcoholic homes. Poverty, racism, the list goes on and on. No matter how polished their pristine outsides look to the starving family in the third world, we are all suffering something. You may think that isn't true, and you have it much worse. Well, I won't deny it. Who on earth can compare sufferings,or understand the mystery of the cross? All I know is that in order to be happy and feel like your life isn't empty, when springtime comes for yet another year, you and I must embrace the cross. We must look up into the sorrowing, loving eyes of Christ, and say with our whole beings: Yes, Lord!! "Thy will be done, thy kingdom come…" That is how you and I will thrive. We turn our lives over to the love and mercy of God. We will trust that God will do something with thismess. He will make it all work out the way He wants.

So, from this day forward, my dear friend and reader, let us, you and me together, thrive! Let us leave all that has happened on the side of the road so to speak. Let's leave our nets, likethe fishermen James, Peter and John, in the Gospels, and follow Jesus, wherever He maylead. All those things we thought were so important; all our dreams, or thoughts about what ourlife was supposed to be, and all the sadness of not having this or that. Please don't think I don'tknow! I do, but whatever we can mourn for is truly earthly. It is all passing anyway. So, let uslong for heaven and look up and adore God with all our might. I know this book isn't foreveryone, but whomever has ears to hear, let him or her hear.

Amen.

Epilogue

In this little booklet I have tried to share my heart with you, dear reader. Some days, evenafter you read this, and after I finished writing it, and maybe even after it gets into your hands, maybe some days will no doubt be hard still. The little things will try to make you and me stumble. But, let us put all that aside now, and realize that all things are trivial distractions from what is really important. Remember, dear friend and reader, when you are in the trenches, you don't care about such little things, as to whether the coffee is hot or cold. Let's just make up our minds, you and me, together, to live for heaven, and shine like blazing lights until that last and final day, when Christ will call us home. Let us live with vitally, not look to the left or right. Let us seize the day, to use a cliché, and let us thrive and be happy in God's divine will, which is everlasting love.

Book Titles

Getting the Truth

By Joseph Koenig

In The Company of Giants: The Ultimate Investigation Guide for Legal Professionals,Journalists, and the Wrongfully Convicted

By Paul J.Ciolino

Uncovering Reasonable Doubt:

The Component MethodBy Brandon

A. Perron